Praise for H

This work, Heart Prints – When Life's Stuff is Tough, is obviously the out-pouring of Cynthia's heart. I felt in this, the palpitation of her heart. And, when one's heart touches another heart, something happens. Something did happen to me. As I read this work, I experienced a pleasant anticipation to keep reading. The style and structure were captivating and intense by her usage of repetitions. The content was most relevant to this world's culture of indifference and brokenness. It is a call back to the Creator and the true meaning of life. Cynthia knows how to broadcast Encouragement and build Hope Towers. I found this to be very Devotional and Motivational in nature and it left me wanting to share it with others. The most moving section of this work, was the last, where she opened her heart about; "My Mother's Love." Thanks Cynthia for sharing your heart with me and the world.

-Ewart F. Brown, motivational and seminar speaker for Building Positive Relationships; author of, A Quiet Place and Love me With Tenderness

Cindy Santiago exposes her heart and soul in, Heart Prints, When Life's Stuff is Tough. With poetry and prose, she takes us on a journey of the emotional roller-coaster of life, with the same emotions and reactions that many of us face every day. Her inspiration is contagious as she faces each challenge with her faith in God. Christian or not, you will be inspired by her words, her conviction, but most of all, her story of victory.

-Albert Fulcher, journalist and editor for The East County Californian

Heart Prints is well written and very touching. I love the poetry. The poems really touched my heart. The ups and downs of life are brought to life in a poem. This book will inspire you through all of the tough things in life that get you down. Cindy's poetry lets the reader know there is hope. Heart Prints leaves a print on your heart as you read it, and it will leave an everlasting print when you finish the book. I think Cindy did wonderful, expressing different hurts in life through her writing. It's 5 star. Heart Prints will help many.

-Diana Montgomery, reviewer

Simple spirituality. Common sense Christianity. Not enough of either in the world. Cindy Santiago's Heart Prints deals with both concepts, leaving the high-flown rhetoric and argumentative theologies that, unfortunately, dog the heels of religious thought. Comprised of poems and a story or two, Heart Prints weaves uncomplicated, everyday stories about everyday things and everyday struggles. If you're looking for epic tales about struggles with faith, this is the wrong book for you. If you want to hear real talk in real time, read Santiago's journey. I promise you'll hear your own voice echoing some of the same questions, same prayers. Heart Prints is about joy, recognition of truth, discovery of a strong inner peace, a way of being that is fueled by doing the hard work that defines a true belief in Divine presence. Santiago shouts, weeps, wonders, reveals, and leads by example. She does the work. So should you. Seeking answers or just now fashioning the questions, this is a book that will set you on the Path. Or, keep your heart and spirit free enough to keep walking.

-Stacy Dyson, poet

Heart Prints

Short Stories & Poems for...

When Life's Stuff is Tough

Cynthia Santiago

This book is dedicated with love to:

My precious mother, Dolores and my devoted aunt Karen.
Thank you for a lifetime of unconditional love.

Blessings

With love and gratitude, I am honored to thank my army of angels

Contents

Introduction
Section One - Fight for the Light

Section Two - It's All God

Section Three - My Mother's Love

Introduction

Writing is my therapy. Through the years I've shared my stories and poems with people who were wounded from life's tough stuff. Ten years ago I began to put this book together with my granddaughter Salina. Originally I called it, "My Heart is an Open Book."

Heart Prints, "When Life's Stuff is Tough," is my collection of passionate poetry and heart-warming prose. Heart Prints is my message of hope. I remind you to reach out for God as you struggle through the toughest times in your life.

When you lose hope, paralyzed in the dark sea of despair, my inspirational words in "Heart Prints," gives you hope to keep swimming. It's tragic that without help, many people lose hope and give up. My wish is that my journey will touch your spirit when you are down, and my truth will leave a print on your heart. My prayer is that my book inspires and motivates you, "When Life's Stuff is Tough."

Section One
Fight for the Light

Cynthia Santiago

Take a Chance

2014

It's not my last chance, but it's a good chance that this time I'll get it right. You see God gave me infinite chances. I've used many, too many to count.

I run away and I come back. I fall down and I get back up. I hate and I forgive. I wrong then I right. I go forward then I go backward. Then I go forward and backward, again and again.

It's not my last chance, but it's a good chance that this time I'll get it right. I won't poison myself with unhealthy living. I won't poison myself with ugly thoughts of negative thinking. It's dangerous you know. It's toxic and it's contagious.

I choose wisdom instead of ignorance. I will replace poison with peace. I will let peace be my guide. I will let peace be my decision maker … "Is this a peaceful decision? Is this a peaceful idea? Is this a peaceful conversation? Do I want a peaceful stroll or a poison train wreck? Am I working with and for the light, or am I giving into the dark?"

It's not my last chance, but it's a good chance that this time I'll get it right. I choose not to be an addict of pain. I choose not to be a misery junky. I choose not to eat, sleep, drink and think poison.

I am a product of my thoughts. I have another chance to think positive. My prayer for you is: Take the chance that God gave you if you want to change. My friend, it's not your last chance, but it's a good chance that this time you will get it right.

Poison I.V.

2004

Remember the poison apple in Snow White?
Be wise my friend, don't take the first bite.
What's your poison? Is it gambling, drugs or booze?
They all control you, and in the end you lose.

You say, "A couple drinks don't make me a boozer.
Losing a few bucks don't mean I'm a loser."
Well, I see it differently, my friend,
If you love poison, you'll lose in the end.

Do you need to get high?
Do you need to fly?
Do you crave a jackpot rush?
The kind you get with a royal flush.
It's poison. . .
Poison makes you sick, poison makes you die.

Poison is a trick; you think you can fly.
What goes up must come down,
Then you need more poison to mask your frown.

Then you run. . .
You run from yourself, you keep running away.
You can't hide what's inside, so you run every day.
You crave the high and get your fix,
You feel real good; it's one of poison's tricks.

You spin. . .
You go around and around as poison's slave,
Then you marry poison and have an early grave.
But you love the dope and you say, "There's no hope."
And you really need poison, it's how you cope.

Poison burns. . .
Friend, it's not worth the price you're payin',
I know you like fun; you think you're just playin'.
But you're playing with fire and with fire you burn,
And always with poison there's a lesson to learn.
You learn and you learn,

You burn and you burn.
Then you say, "I'll quit."
But you take another hit.

It's a roller coaster ride. . .
You're hooked on the poison high,
You can't say good-bye.
Then one day you're tired of the spin,
You realize with poison you never win.
Poison is a vicious ride,
Poison is a razor blade slide.

And you get tired. . .
When you've had enough and if you're wise you will,
Realize poison is just a phony thrill.
When you're tired of the high and the low,
When you're tired of the fast and the slow,
When you're tired of the love and the hate,
When you're tired of poison for your date,
You will get wise.

It's a choice. . .
Ignorant or wise, ignorant or wise,
Poison wears a fun disguise.
Poison is a lie and I'll tell you why,
Poison isn't real, it numbs how you feel.

Poison Control . . .
Poison whispers, "Come to me."
Then poison lies about reality.
So now you know because I told you so,
Poison isn't the way to go.
So what do you do? Easier said than done,
Talk is cheap and you like having fun.

Time to pray . . . time to talk to God.
Can you replace poison? Can you replace it with love?
Can you love you and not do what you do?
Can you swim and not sink?
Can you not take another drink?
Can you resist poison's lure?
Can you pray to reach out for a cure?

Ask God to help you today?
Then you can finally throw poison away.
Pray to God when you're feeling low,
God will give you strength to just say, "NO!"

Nowhere Train

2009

"All aboard!" the devil said,
So I climbed the steps with my empty head.
A train to nowhere, I can ride,
A train to nowhere, I can hide.
I sat still in the eerie quiet,
This train to nowhere, I will try it.

With a blast my train left fast,
In seconds, I faced my past.
I gazed out the window to a blur,
It broke my heart, "The way we were."
I cried, then I wiped my nose with my shirt,
I cried 'cause my broken heart still hurt.

On this high speed nowhere train,
It seemed that I was going insane.
No one on the train understood,
No one on the train could.
On a nowhere train, no one cared,
On this nowhere train, I was scared.
I boarded the train to run away,
Soon I learned I didn't want to stay.
The nowhere train wore a fun disguise,
The nowhere train was built with lies.
I got sick traveling nowhere miles,
I got tired of smiling empty smiles.
The nowhere train went around and around,
"STOP the train, I want homeward bound!"
No one listened, no one heard,
I wanted it to stop, it was absurd.

I wanted off the nowhere train,
I wanted God to ease my pain.
I wanted off the train right now,
I wanted it to stop, but I didn't know how.

The nowhere train going the wrong way,
Knocked me on my knees to pray.
Then my heart exploded when I heard God say,
"You ignored My love so you went astray."
Then God stopped the train with, "My Will Be Done."
God touched me, "You forgot the blood of My Son."
"No sorrow for today and tomorrow, I love you" God said,
"Remember life is good, not something to dread."
I trembled when God carried me off the train.
I thanked Him for His love and for healing my pain.

Crazy

2012

I know crazy.
You want crazy?
I know crazy.

Adrenaline, bubbling rage!
I know crazy.
You want crazy?
I know crazy.

Yes, I know crazy.
Crazy doesn't think.
Crazy will cut your throat,
Crazy will hurt you in a blink.
You want crazy?

Crazy is from hell,
Crazy is not well.
Crazy is from pain,
Crazy makes you insane.
I know crazy.

Crazy goes to jail,
Crazy don't make bail.
Crazy won't leave,
Crazy can't breathe.
I know crazy.

Crazy can't cope,
Crazy don't hope.
Crazy can't see,
Crazy is me. . .

When
I
don't
pray.

I know pray,
You need to pray?
I know pray.

I know pray,
I know how to pray crazy away.
I know pray.
Pray is here to stay.

I know pray.
You need to pray?
I know God,
God told me to pray.

God turns crazy to calm.
God turns mad to glad.
God turns hate to love.
God turns frowns to smiles.
God turns darkness to light.
God makes everything alright.

I know God and I know love.
When I'm crazy, I forget what I know,
I take a deep breath,
And I pray for crazy to go.

God is the way when you're lost,
God is the way when you're sad, mad, or crazy.
I know what I know.
God is the way, so pray and you'll be okay.

This One's for Me

1981

She's always written about things she's done,
She'll share one secret that wasn't much fun.
"It started a couple months ago," she said,
Depression took over and shook her head.

She battled it, then was okay for a while,
It would strike again, she couldn't smile.
She felt like she was Jekyll and Hyde,
One day she laughed, one day she cried.

Some days she felt empty, forced herself to speak,
Broke glass and broke hearts, help she refused to seek.
She hated herself, disliked her husband and her child,
Only thing that made her happy was completely going wild.

She'd return to calm, then guilt from breaking hearts,
"Sorry," was painful with promising better starts.
Pressure in her head is how she described the attack,
She told her mom it was like a monkey on her back.

She tried to solve it, just normal problems in life,
Wondering why it was so hard to be a mother and a wife.
Often things from the past crept up, then she'd dwell,
Didn't take long, monkey jumped on, she was back in self-made hell.

Everything got her down and made her worry,
Even if she wasn't going anywhere, she was always in a hurry.
She didn't have to argue with anyone, inside her was a fight,
It was hard to be good, easy to be bad, while trying to find the light.

One day when hatred took over, her husband put a mirror in her face,
Once sweet as an angel now a vicious devil was the case.
She knew something had to be done; she couldn't take it anymore,
It crossed her mind that God could open the door.

She complained daily, she was always mad,
Desperate she searched for the happiness she once had.
Sorrow from inner problems buried deep,
With constant nightmares, never a good night's sleep.

She prayed for comfort and guidance from above,
Easter soon played a part, the message of eternal love.
Self-control, a gift from God, a responsibility,
She chose to be peaceful and enjoy living you see.

She found pleasure in her family; her heart once again, carried a song,
She wondered how this life so right, once seemed so very wrong.
She'll never forget that monkey; he'll try her off and on,
When she feels his pressure, she prays and he is gone.

It used to be each day was a day she'd dread,
After praying to God she regained a clear head.
If you get confused with problems you can't bear,
Please ask God for help, you know He'll always care.

I'm Back

2008

I'm back, I'm finally back from far away,
I'm back, and I've got something good to say.
My friend, I escaped from Hell,
The truth is, I wasn't very well.

Yes, I'm back but I will never forget,
When I fell into Hell's dark pit.
I fell and I fell, I fell down so low,
No one could help me, it was dark you know.
I cried and I tried and I screamed inside,
Then I lost hope on Hell's razor blade ride.

So I sat in the darkness of Hell,
And I looked how far I had fell.
I was mad and sad, I couldn't think.
It was useless so I took another drink.

Hell fed me drugs, and booze, and lies,
Hell had everything, even maggots and flies.
I hated the stink and the dark,
But when I cried, Hell's vicious dogs would bark.

So badly, I wanted to leave,
"I WANT OUT, SOMEONE HELP ME," I'd grieve.
Then in my heart, I heard a soft voice,
But I ignored it; again, I made the wrong choice.
I heard that voice through the years,
But I ignored it and focused on my tears.

Then a miracle happened one night,
The voice said, "I love you," I will fight your fight.
I cried, "Can you get me out of this grave?"
The voice said, "Yes, your life I will save."

With dirty hands, I cried, "What do I do?"
The voice said, "Love me and I'll take care of you."
"But what if I drown in this quicksand?"
The voice answered back, "Trust me, just take my hand."
I cried, "Who are you, I'm so scared?"
The voice said, "I am God, now your life is spared."

"Thank you," I cried, and God heard,
I prayed and He showed me His word.
Then I saw a light, a beautiful light,
God revealed my soul, shining so bright.
God gave me a key; He said, "Just trust Me."
I unlocked Hell's gate, and I was free.

So I'm back, I'm finally back, from far away,
I'm back and I've got something good to say.
If you are lost, so very lost today,
Trust God; trust Him to show you the way.

Handcuffs

2010

My hands are cuffed behind my back,
My hair is in my eyes.
My hands are cuffed behind my back,
I can't swat the flies.

My hands are cuffed behind my back,
And I don't have the key.
My hands are cuffed behind my back,
I struggle to be free.

My hands are cuffed behind my back,
My thoughts keep me down.
My hands are cuffed behind my back,
My mind and hands are bound.

My hands are cuffed behind my back,
My body feels the pain.
My hands are cuffed behind my back,
. . . shackled to my brain.

My hands are cuffed behind my back,
I can't sing my song.
My hands are cuffed behind my back,
I wonder for how long.

My hands are cuffed behind my back,
There's nothing I can do.
My hands are cuffed behind my back,
If only God knew.

Then God said:
"Your hands are cuffed behind your back,
There's something you should know.
Your hands are cuffed behind your back,
It's time for you to grow.

Your hands are cuffed behind your back,
And since you wonder why,
Your hands are cuffed behind your back,
Again you must try.

Your hands are cuffed behind your back,
Faith will let you see.
Your hands are cuffed behind your back,
So you will search for Me."

I thanked God for unlocking my handcuffs,
He said, "Always surrender the fight."
It's hard, but with God I can do it,
Even when my handcuffs are tight.

The Dove

1988

Once upon a time, but not so long ago, lived a mother. She had a bad day that was a sad day, but nobody knew. She smiled though she hurt. She laughed though she cried inside. Nothing, but everything was on her mind. She got up on the wrong side of the world and she couldn't cope with life.

She should have talked about her problems, but she didn't. Talking is therapeutic, but who cares? She was a functioning robot, living but not alive. Did you ever have one of those days? Did you ever have one of those months?

Pain fogged her brain so she couldn't see beyond her nose. A pit bull *locked his jaw* around her mind...she wanted to run but there was nowhere to hide. Did you ever feel like running away?

20

It was the same story a different day. The repetition of life was getting her down. Have you ever stopped to think how much you repeat yourself? How you repeat what you do every day? Day after day, week after week, year after year, we repeat what we do.

The mother was depressed and thinking too much about all the wrong things. She forgot to count her blessings. She forgot to be positive. She lost her smile and her spirit. She forgot how to console herself. She fell down and Band-Aids were nowhere to be found.

Later that afternoon, at the beach, the disturbed mother met a white-winged dove. The angelic dove radiated love. The tiny dove was wise. She knew exactly what to say.

The dove said, "So you feel like running away?" The mother's eyes filled with tears. "Yes," she cried, "I'm confused about life. There's more pain than pleasure."

"Oh, no, you're wrong," the dove insisted, "Life is good and life is worth living. The fog will lift and you'll see clearly again."

The mother listened as the dove preached, "Quit beating yourself up. Control your thoughts. Don't let your thoughts control you. Relax, because this too shall pass. Soon you'll feel better. A bright light will show you the way. Just have faith."

A few days later the mother stumbled into the light. She was alive! Inspiration melted the lock that had imprisoned her mind. Confusion and pain vanished. Confidence and self-esteem returned. Her joyful spirit was back. Hope danced in her heart. Life made sense again. She thanked God that peace found the rainbow in her heart.

Press On

1982

Sunshine, blue skies
    Birds chirp, shoo flies
        Faint breeze, green leaves

Hot summer day
    Sunburn dismay
        My mind astray
            While children play

Our lives on hold
    Though love is gold
        The world seems cold

Time will tell
    Waiting is Hell
        Prayers heard

No job word
    It's absurd

Useless outcry
    Wondering why
        Weeks go by
            Hard we try

Remind Me Again

1988

I gaze in my mirror and see,
A Christian, a good heart, carefree.

Yet wondering if I lost the key,
Today there's no fight left in me.

I'm too weak for more combat,
Though I keep faith, I have lots of that.
Again on my face I fell flat,
Kicked while down by the cruel Hellcat.

So I pity myself, I'm blue,
Then fed my depression and it grew.
I was burnt at his barbeque,
Mere snack on the devil's menu.

To give in for a while was alright,
As I couldn't find strength to fight.
If I pray will it help, it might?
I didn't throw in the towel, not quite.

I prayed and asked, "God did you know?
The Hellcat devoured me real slow,
And I fought but he wouldn't let me go."
God smiled, "With each struggle you grow."

Human means sometimes giving in,
God reminded me that it's no sin.
I'll grin and pick up my chin,
Learning every fight I won't win.

23

Misery Wants Company

2012

Misery visits without an invitation. Misery stays too long and paralyzes its victim. Misery, like a maggot, eats hope. Misery slowly kills. Misery steals energy, confidence, and spirit. Misery devours faith and poisons love. Misery corrupts the mind and the emotions of the miserable. Misery blindfolds the miserable so they stumble, fall and quit trying.

If you are giving up, distraught in your thoughts, take off your blindfold. Get up; switch quit to quiet, and paralyzed for prayer. Pray, "God turn my darkness to light and show me that misery is a mirage."

You can do it! Evict misery, conquer being miserable. It's victory for the victim. Set your soul free.

Satan's Sticky Spider Web

2012

My eyes were wide open, but I didn't see,
When the wicked Satan spider spun his web on me.
I fought and fought and fought to get free,
The more I fought, I got distraught.
I was mad and sad, it was really bad.
. . . I couldn't move.

When I got tired of fighting,
And tired of the spider biting. . . ME!
I yelled out, SE-CUR-ITY! SE-CUR-ITY!

I bled from my head,
I wished I was dead.
So I yelled, "SE-CUR-ITY!" once more.

My vision was blurred,
When a voice I heard.
My mind and heart knew,
As He came into view,
Jesus asked, "Can I help you?"

Though they were covered with flies,
 I couldn't believe my eyes.
His shirt said, "SECURITY, I'll set you free."

Just when my future looked grim,
My hands shook as I reached for Him.
Weak, I whispered, "What took you so long?"
He wiped my eyes, "I love you, I need you strong."

Never Quit

1973

Life was too painful when I was blind,
Running away and quitting was always on my mind.
I stumbled in the dark, I couldn't walk.
I almost called God, but I couldn't talk.

I hated life, I planned to leave,
I thought God would bless those who grieve.
Then an angel called my name,
And I'll never be the same.
In the dark where there's no light,
I saw a rainbow shining bright.

With God's love, I can clearly see,
God has a plan, especially for me.
Thank you God, You lit my bottomless pit,
You have my word, I'll never quit.

27

Backslide

2003

It felt like a fun ride,
Again to myself I lied.
I didn't plan to backslide,
Then I had no place to hide.

God knows how hard I tried,
But "Temptation Road" is wide.
The road wears a fun disguise,
A dead-end paved with lies.

The end of the road was dark,
It wasn't where I wanted to park.
I've been to the end before,
My heart can't take it no more.

That dark road I won't return,
I know the pain of backslide burn.
One huge lesson I did learn,
Next time I'll make the right turn.

Patience

1984

Once in the mud I was stuck,
I might have known, just my luck.
My eyes were wide open, not closed,
I had mud from my head to my toes.

I figured I was destined to rot,
I lost control so hard I fought.
I swore and struggled to be free,
Rage made a wildcat of me.

A mess, I was drained and distraught,
Then silence spoke of what I forgot.
I paused to hear not a sound,
God lifted my heart off the ground.

God, thank you, I'm out of the mud,
How could I forget Your son's blood?
I won't let evil destroy my mind,
Your love has taught me to be kind.

Shake, Surrender, Soar

2003

When someone hurts you, shake it off,
When someone gets in your space,
 Or gets in your face,
Shake it off.

When someone hurts you,
Don't be glue and let it stick to you.
Shake it off.

Though it may sound odd,
Shake it off and give it to God.

Surrender the pain,
So you can regain,
Your balance.

When someone slams your heart's door,
Don't fall down on the floor,
Shake it off, surrender, soar.

I'm On My Way

2013

My dear friend, my rowboat used to spin and spin and it wasn't spinning from the wind.

Satan had his evil hand on my little boat and continued to flick my boat with his wicked finger. So around and around I went. I was sick. I was dizzy. I was confused. I was distraught because I forgot what I know. I got black and blue from spinning.

Then, one very dark, cold, lonely night, I lost my fight. I lost my soul and I lost sight of my goal. I gave up. I didn't have a clue what to do. I couldn't paddle my boat straight, it was too late. My hands had sores, I lost my oars. I planned to quit and jump ship. No matter how much I begged, Satan wouldn't let my little boat go.

I was tired. I was afraid and I was cold. I didn't care about living. I felt hopeless. I was about to jump in the deep ocean of good-bye. With evil thoughts I stood in my spinning boat. I couldn't take the spin. I couldn't win. I couldn't stand the pain and I couldn't explain. No one understood. No one could ... I was ready to jump.

Suddenly I heard words. I heard words in my mind. Tears rolled down my face as I fought to keep my balance. "Say it!" echoed in my head, "Say it!" So I shouted to Heaven, "IN THE NAME OF JESUS, SATAN TAKE YOUR HAND OFF MY BOAT! IN THE NAME OF JESUS, SATAN TAKE YOUR HAND OFF MY BOAT!"

Immediately my little boat stopped spinning. The darkness became light. Bewildered, I sat down. My oars were back. I could see my way. I wasn't dizzy. I wasn't sick. I wasn't cold or afraid. And I wasn't alone.

Jesus told me, "You are not alone. You were never alone. I love you now and I loved you then. I am your only forever friend to the end."

I was used during my time spent with Satan. I was used and confused, battered and bruised . . . But I was never alone.

My dear friend, I say, "Keep hope rowing your boat." I pray you get from here to there. I pray you remember that God does care. I pray you row with me and we smile in the sun. I pray and know we will make it because we are the chosen ones.

So, I'm in my rowboat paddling across life from here to there. I'm not afraid. I'm not cold and I'm not tired. It's a long, long journey from here to there, but I'll make it.

You see my faithful rowboat is finally going one way, the right way, and the light way. I will get there this time. From here to there is far, oh so far, too far for my car. So as I paddle and pray, I smile and tell God, "I'm on my way."

Darkness

1970

My mind's on replay
    Ugly yesterday
        Pain cut my heart
            Lives drift apart

Someone I know
    Let the devil show
        Beating my brain
            Tears fell like rain

Patience was few
    As hatred grew
        Push came to shove
            No sign of love

Dazed and confused
    Feeling abused
        Nowhere to hide
            Hurting inside

I Broke Up With Jesus

2014

I broke up with Jesus, I went on my way,
I didn't care I had no rhyme that day.
I didn't plan to be bad, mad, or sad,
I didn't think about the good thing we had.

I broke up with Jesus, my head was not well,
My eyes did not see I was headed to Hell.
I didn't hear our song, I didn't think about
His love lifelong.

I broke up with Jesus, I went insane,
With a knife in my heart I only knew pain.
I broke up with Jesus, I didn't behave,
I lost my head and dug my own grave.

Yes, I broke up with Jesus, but I missed Him today,
I cried out, "Jesus I need you, I didn't mean to stray!"

"Jesus do you hear me?" I fell to my knees,
"Jesus forgive me, forgive me please!"
Jesus healed my head and blessed my heart,
He said, "My child we were never apart."

He smiled, "I love you, you're alright.
Lost in the dark you found my light."
Jesus said, "My child you forgot what you knew,
You always need me when you're black and blue."
"My child, don't look back," Jesus said,
"Forgive and go forward with My love instead."

Grief

2008

The struggle to live without my precious mother is an ongoing process. I wrote about grieving to help myself and to help you cope if you have lost someone you love.

I find grief harder than I imagined. The resurfacing thing keeps knocking me out. What I learned, I will share with you. We all grieve differently.

Grief is **INVISIBLE** to others. Others do not know your heart is still breaking.

Others do not remember your continuous struggle to cope with your loss. Be patient with family and friends.

Grief **RESURFACES**. When you least expect it, grief resurfaces and knocks you out again. Grief resurfacing is torture. Right when you are sailing through your day, it happens. Like a rollercoaster there are highs and lows.

And, there are **TURBULENT MOMENTS!** I still wash my face with tears like a little girl. Grief is personal. Don't be too hard on yourself. Don't expect too much too soon. Grief is a FOG. You cannot see clearly in fog. If you go too fast in the fog you crash. If you do; pick yourself up, brush yourself off and know the fog will lift. This too shall pass.

You are **NORMAL**. Crying uncontrollably is normal. Not crying is normal. Whatever you are doing is right for you. But, do **HELP YOURSELF** by sharing the pain when it is unbearable. Talking to your loved one is normal.

The **first year** is the hardest. All firsts are heart-bursts. The first holidays are torture without your loved one. You need to be with people that love you and care. It's okay to fall apart.

There are **TRIGGERS**. A variety of things trigger our emotions. Songs make you cry. Other songs make you smile. Reading cards or letters they wrote to you could be bittersweet. You miss them. Your heart aches for them. Even your sense of smell can be a trigger. Smelling their perfume or cologne brings back memories that trigger emotions.

Your relationship with your loved one has **transformed**. Now it's a therapeutic relationship. Talking to your loved one is positive. Believing they hear you is faith.

Knowing they are happy is the **TRUTH**. Trust God and know you will see your loved one again.

Their **legacy** is important. Keep your loved one's memory alive. Tell their story. Share with those who care.

When you are ready, revisit the places you enjoyed together. If it's comforting, wear their clothing or jewelry to remind you of them. I wear my mother's cross.

Grief is **a painful place to be**. Grief is paralyzing to the one grieving. Grief is an individual thing. Sometimes we walk. Other times we crawl. Sometimes we get stuck. Some people stop moving. Some people don't want to go on. If you don't want to go on, you are in crisis. Reach out. People love you and people do care.

There are **STAGES** of grief. The stages range from shock to anger, guilt, denial, and depression. In time the last stage is acceptance. Not everyone goes through each stage and not necessarily in that order.

The task of **MOURNING** begins with accepting you've had a loss. Then you must work (live) through the pain. The next task is becoming adjusted to your environment without the person you love. Last, but not least, you emotionally relocate your relationship with them. They are not gone, they are away.

The task of mourning does not come in a timeframe. They are guidelines to help. It is a process. It is about not giving up. It is about going on.

God bless you if you are hurting because someone you love is away. Your life has changed. Take your time.

One day you will smile. One day you will dance. And, my friend, one day you will meet again. Take care of yourself.

A Boy and His Wagon

1990

For Dorothy Rumsey & Conni Cotter Benham

Once upon a time there lived a happy little boy. He had a brand new red wagon.

He and his wagon were inseparable. Oh how he loved his wagon.

Then one day cruel bullies harassed the boy. They took his wagon to use and abuse it. They broke his wagon and broke his heart.

The little boy was sad. The bullies heckled and tormented him. He cried when they called him a sissy. They threw the broken wagon at him.

As fast as he could, he pulled his broken wagon home. It's a wonder it rolled on three wheels. The wagon was dented and ugly. The little boy was hurt.

He was determined to fix his wagon. He took his time and he fixed it with nobody's help. It looked better. It rolled smooth again. He was alright.

But time after time the big bullies returned to break him and break his wagon. One day they tore off every wheel and severely dented the body. They twisted the handle until it snapped. The nice little boy became very angry. He fought. He lost. They laughed. He raged. He was tired of fighting and tired of losing. Once again he carried a broken wagon and a broken heart.

He controlled his pain with anger. He was mad at the bullies, mad at his wagon, and mad at himself. He could no longer fix it. He dropped the wagon in the backyard. He ignored his feelings of loss and sadness.

Some days he'd approach the pitiful wagon. If he started to cry, he'd kick it in a fit of rage. He'd throw it against the fence and roar, "I hate them!"

Time went by and winter rain rusted the wagon. No sign of shiny red paint. No sign of a once happy boy.

"I don't need any help! I don't care about that stupid wagon! Just leave me alone!" he'd shout.

But he needed help, as he truly cared about his precious wagon. He was confused. He didn't understand and he couldn't cope.

Pieces of his wagon were lost throughout the yard. The broken wheels were here, the bent handle was there and the rusted body was someplace else. His dream wagon was a nightmare.

The boy continued to get sadder and angrier, yet never sought help. He couldn't.

He felt useless and empty like his wagon. He became extremely ill. If he didn't accept help soon, he would die.

A wise old teacher visited the sick boy. The old man sat on the edge of the boy's bed and looked deep into his eyes. "My son, you are very sick. You need my help. Please trust me to help you get better."

"NO!" The child refused and yelled, "I'm not sick! Just leave me alone!"

The wise man replied, "Wounded child, sad child, I have the tools to fix you and your wagon."

He continued, "Together we will pick up the pieces. As we rebuild your wagon, we will rebuild you. I care about you and I care about your wagon."

The boy was scared, he cried hysterically. He didn't think he was strong enough. He didn't think he could do it.

The wise man gently took the boy's hand. Slowly they entered the backyard. The boy started to cry and walk away. The wise man caught him and hugged him tight. "You'll be fine. I'm with you. Now help me find all the wagon pieces. You must feel to heal.

Someday you will understand."

It wasn't easy. With patience and prayers, the young boy and the old man took the first step of the long journey. They collected wagon parts and broken hearts. As they restored the wagon the boy regained strength. They pounded dents and sanded rust. They fixed the bent handle and attached it.

Then, on went the wheels. Step by step, piece by piece, painfully, yet joyfully, the wagon was coming together . . . as was the child.

Next up, was the shiny red paint and black on the handle. It was unbelievable. No visible scars. The boy could smile. He even whistled.

While the paint dried, the teacher said, "The wagon is yours and only yours. The bullies were sick and they caused your sickness. But now you're getting better, and with my help you will learn to forgive them."

The old man and the boy became close friends. One afternoon as they walked, pulling the shiny red wagon, they talked. The boy asked his wise friend, "Why did you help me?"

The gentle man paused and softly set his hand on the boy's shoulder, "My beloved son, once upon a time, many, many years ago, when I was your age, I had a little red wagon . . . just like yours.

Dry Your Tear

1980

Upon my death, when I die,
Comfort each other, please try.
Leaving is the hardest step to take,
Left is the living with painful heartache.

With memories, your mind is unclear,
Hard to believe I could disappear.
Realize I'm gone, God called my name,
Heaven is life, no suffering or pain.

Sad for you, I was here yesterday,
My smile, my laugh, and the things I'd say.
Give thanks for love, our time together,
I'll remain in your heart forever.

Something you can anticipate,
Blessings come to those who wait.
Patience my dear, have faith not fear,
We'll rejoice in Heaven, dry your tear.

Section Two
It's All God

Cynthia Santiago

Stand Tall

2010

Children come and children go,
Children play and children grow.
Children smile when they're loved it's true,
How's the child that lives in you?

How's your child of yesterday?
Is your inner child okay?
Is your inner child glad or sad?
Is your inner child doing good or bad?

Some children are told to be seen and not heard,
Some children were afraid and spoke not a word.
Some children didn't have a voice,
Some children didn't have a choice.

Yes, children laugh and children cry,
And little children wonder why.
Some parents are nice and some are mean,
Some are a child's nightmare, but some are a dream.

Then parents and children and seasons change,
Children become parents, isn't it strange?
The life cycle begins again,
Some children lose and some children win.

Stand tall if your inner child was confused,
Stand tall if your inner child was abused.
Stand tall if you were scarred in childhood,
Stand tall even if no one understood.

Stand tall to protect the ones you love,
Stand tall to the bullies that continue to shove.
Stand tall when you want to run and hide,
Stand tall when your child cries inside.

Stand tall when your life makes no sense,
Stand tall when you fall off the fence.
And next time someone makes you feel small,
Remember you're God's child, stand tall!

The Rest is Up to You

2009

For Betty Henderlite

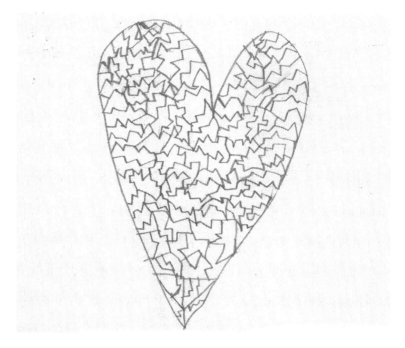

I was walking on the beach. I was just walking and thinking . . . then, suddenly from behind, I felt a tap on my shoulder. Shocked, I turned around . . . I shrieked, "Oh my God!" I couldn't believe I was looking at Jesus . . . tears rolled down my face. I was speechless . . . I thought I was going to die.

Jesus asked me, "Did you lose this?" He had something in His hand. I didn't understand, because I didn't think I had lost anything. As I wiped my nonstop tears, I watched as Jesus slowly opened His hand. He was *holding my heart*. I froze and I listened.

Jesus told me, "I knew this was yours when I found it. It was broken, but you need your heart." I cried, "I didn't realize I had lost it. I didn't realize it was gone."

Jesus explained, "You've been losing it little by little through the years. Every time you are hurt, every time you feel pain, every time you lose control; you lose a little bit of your heart without even realizing it."

"I have fixed your broken heart," Jesus smiled. "I have filled the cracks with My love. I have mended the scars with My blood. I give you this new heart and I give you a new start. The rest is up to you."

God's Gift

2011

God has a gift for you,
He taped you when you didn't know.
He recorded every day of your life,
So you'll have your very own show.

Yes, God has a gift for you,
He recorded you day and night.
He saw every move you made,
In the dark and in the light.

God has a gift for you,
He's been watching you since your birth.
He never left your side,
And He'll be with you when you leave this earth.

God has a gift for you,
He'll show you on judgment day.
Then you and God will quietly watch,
As the angels rejoice and pray.

Rainbows Forever

1981

When you're down, trust God and climb.
Step by step, life takes time.
The road's rough, you'll stumble and crawl.
Take God's hand, when you fall.

Flat on your face, you hurt bad,
Your heart is confused, empty, and sad.
Angry tears, wondering why,
Neglecting God's watchful eye.

Take a silent moment or two.
Say a prayer, God loves you.
When you don't think you'll survive,
Think twice, thank God you're alive.

My friend, next climb, next steep hill,
Pray that you'll make it, soon you will.
On dark days, if you see no sun,
Remember Jesus, the chosen one.

Direction

1984

Are you lost with nowhere to turn?
So many answers you seek to learn?
Your mind is dizzy, your head's in a spin.
Dear, Jesus is where you begin.

Pray He'll guide you through this storm,
He'll forever keep your heart warm.
In His hands you will always remain.
He'll dry your tears; He'll ease your pain.

Cynthia Santiago

I Have a Date With God

2004

As I anticipate my special date
It will be great, I can't be late
It means a lot to me
God is who I'll see
I have a date with God

God said, "Practice what you preach
Come see me at my beach
Watch the seagulls fly
Admire my blue sky"

I have a date with God
Because life is on my mind
God whispered, "Be still
Answers you will find"

I have a date with God
So don't get in my way
I've kept God waiting long enough
That's all I have to say.

Time to Open Your Gifts

2011

Dance when no one is dancing;
Sing when no one sings;
Care when no one cares;
Help when no one helps;
Love when no one loves;
Be still when no one is still;
Forgive when no one forgives;

In dancing and singing, caring and helping,
Your spirit is joyful.
In loving, in stillness, and in forgiving,
Your spirit soars like an eagle above the pain.

Smile when no one smiles;
Hug when no one hugs;
Give when no one gives;
Pray when no one prays.

Smiling, hugging, giving and praying are gifts from God. . .
It's time to open your gifts.

Did You?

2012

For Sandi Provence

Jesus asked, "Did you stop loving me? Did you stop trusting me? Did you stop having faith in Me?"

I was speechless. My tears flowed as I tried to swallow. Words wouldn't come out of my mouth.

I looked at Jesus. I got on my knees. I didn't know what to say or how to say it. I just cried.

Jesus touched my head and asked me, "Did you forget I love you? Did you forget you love me? Did you forget I'm waiting?"

My body trembled. I began to sweat. My hands shook. My tears were nonstop. My voice was silent.

I thought, "How can I answer? How can I make Him understand?" I have no excuse for my distance from Him. I have no excuse for my behavior. I have no words to express my sorrow and my shame.

Jesus asked, "Did you run the other way? Did you forget to pray? Did you stumble in the night, did you forget My light?"

I was numb with guilt. I agonized, "How can I repay the debt I owe to Him?" I was

paralyzed by pain, because Jesus and I had had this conversation so many times before.

Now what? I was embarrassed. I was ashamed, I was sorry … again. So I took a deep breath and I wiped my eyes.

Jesus said, "I love you, and I will always love you. I have a gift for you." I wondered what it could be. I am blessed. I have so many blessings. What more could Jesus give me?

Then Jesus said, "Open your hand." He placed a folded piece of paper in my hand. I opened it -- and written with His blood -- I read these words:

"My child, I love you, even when you stray, I love you. I love you unconditionally. Did you know you are forgiven? . . . Paid in full."

Imagine That

2008

Imagine not worrying too much. Imagine not hurrying or caring too much. Imagine having only nice things to say. Imagine life with smiles and no frowns. Imagine your best friend is always around. Imagine that loved ones never leave. Imagine never having to grieve. Imagine life with no sadness or pain. Imagine rainbows when you walk in the rain. Imagine your heart never hurts that bad. Imagine that your days aren't all sad. Imagine *that*.

Imagine with every good-bye around the corner there's a sweet, "Hi." Imagine the road that you once traveled, is merely your blanket that's now unraveled. You walked years of roads and many miles under your feet. Then you opened a gate and you crossed a street. Imagine *that*.

Imagine that you sat alone in the sand. Then a special friend took your hand. Imagine the work you do and the mountains you climb. And it doesn't matter if you don't have a rhyme. Imagine *that*.

Imagine climbing with tears and facing your fears on your new road. And your unraveled blanket in a heap, is the cherished old road and something you keep. Imagine *that*.

But it's a new day and it's a new road. Imagine new courage to climb with this new load. Your load is heavy and the road a steep hill. Some will help and others stand still. Some make your load heavy and some make your load light. But you carry your load in spite of the fight. Imagine *that*.

Imagine that you walk and you fall. And sometimes your road is no fun at all. Imagine **really** trusting God as your guide. Imagine never having to hide. Imagine remembering the **good** not the bad. Imagine the happy not the sad. Imagine *that*.

So my friend, I'm telling you…imagine on your road I'm praying for you. And when you fall, give me a call. I'll be there. I do care. Imagine we can walk and talk. Together we will climb. My friend we will take one step at a time. Imagine **that!**

Walking Wounded

2009

God bless the walking wounded,
They pray that no one knows.
God bless the walking wounded,
Cause the wound they cover shows.

God bless the walking wounded,
You see them walk in war.
God bless the walking wounded,
You see them at the store.

God bless the walking wounded,
They walk without a smile.
God bless the walking wounded,
Pray for them awhile.

God bless the walking wounded,
With a pain they try to hide.
God bless the walking wounded,
And all the tears they've cried.

God bless the walking wounded,
Know their pain is real.
God bless the walking wounded,
Pray their pain will heal.

God bless the walking wounded,
In their silent hell;
God bless the walking wounded,
Pray they soon get well.

God bless the walking wounded,
They walk slowly it is true.
God bless the walking wounded,
It could be me, it could be you.

Cynthia Santiago

A Cup of Quiet

2005

Enjoy a cup of quiet
Don't mind if I do
For in my cup of quiet
I'll spend some time with you

Have one cup of quiet
It's good to the last drop
Sip your cup of quiet
Take time from life to stop

I love my cup of quiet
And friend I'll tell you why
Stop to smell the roses
Before the roses die

Try a cup of quiet
If you've been stressed
You deserve a cup of quiet
One sip and you are blessed.

You Belong to Him

2011

Your future's looking grim,
You feel you never win.
Because you forgot . . . again,
You belong to Him.

You're tired; you've cried and tried,
So you decide to run and hide.
But you didn't stop to look inside,
You belong to Him.

When you do what's not good to do,
You're miserable, isn't it true?
With a heart that's black and blue,
You belong to Him.

You belong to the Lord,
He'll protect you with His sharp sword.
Even when His love you ignored,
You belong to Him.

He forgives you when you're not wise,
And He'll wait 'til you open your eyes.
Then you will clearly see,
He will set your heart free.

You belong to Him.

God Does Care

1981

When things in life don't work when they should,
You get disgusted, you wish they would.
Drowning yourself with pain and sorrow,
You wonder if things will change tomorrow.

When you're confused and problems don't end,
Pray to God, He's always your friend.
Open your heart, clear your mind.
Anxiety will leave, harmony you'll find.

We're all God's children, don't you fret,
Ask Him in prayer, answers you'll get.
When you worry and life seems unfair,
Fear not, have faith, God does care.

Don't Hide

1984

Praise the Lord, child sing,
You're safe under God's wing.
His love surrounds you,
Trust Him child, it's true.

Praise the Lord, little peach,
You'll not bruise when you reach.
Be the best on the tree,
Wink at the honey bee.

Praise the Lord every day,
Forever with you He will stay.
Don't hide from rain on your head,
Praise His rainbow instead.

God's Eyes

2010

God was watching you yesterday,
He watched you as you went on your way.
He remembered when you were very small,
He even remembers your first bad fall.

Then as God had your life in His view,
He gave His unconditional love to you.
God blessed you as He watched what you did,
He saw how you've grown since you were a kid.

When God was watching you the other night,
He loved what He saw, you're doing alright.
God said, "You're grown up, but when you fall,
You forget Me, you forget to call."

Every day God watches you out of His eyes,
Remember He sees through your ego disguise.
But He also sees your heart so wise,
And He continues to help through your many tries.

If you could see yourself as God sees you,
You would live each day and know it's new.
You would soar like an eagle and run like a deer,
See with God's eyes, because His eyes are clear.

Cynthia Santiago

Believe

1984

Last night I watched you cry,
You cried out, "Why, God why?"
I sat on the edge of your bed,
And saw every tear you shed.

You asked, "What has God done for me?"
My child, if you would only see.
I continue to offer My hand,
You bury your head in quicksand.

If you'd come up for air,
I'd show you that I care.
I promise to set your heart free,
I'll listen, confide in Me.

Child, I'll take all your scars,
And turn them into stars.
It's time you realize,
You must open your eyes.

63

Take a really long look,
View nature's babbling brook.
Mountains, oceans, My blue sky,
Insects, flowers, hummingbirds fly.

How can you ignore My love?
Or doubt the Heaven's above.
I gave My only Son,
Proof My will be done.
Believe in Me, confess, I'll forgive,
Eternal life you will live.

Evidence

1984

"I will rise," Jesus said,
On the cross as He bled.
"Child, don't weep when I'm dead.
Rejoice Heaven's ahead."

There were doubts and dismay,
Troubled hearts would pray.
So astonished were they. . .
He appeared the third day.

Standing before their eyes,
He kept His promise to arise.
He set rainbows in the sky,
To remind us He's close by.

Count Your Blessings

1984

Count your blessings sad child,
Instead of going wild.
Realize God's gifts for you,
Pray and praise Him too.

Count your blessings, child don't frown,
Pick your heart up off the ground.
Confused child, God is the key,
To love, joy and harmony.

Count your blessings, child smile,
Thank dear God awhile.
Give the Lord your hand,
Forever with you He'll stand.

Count your blessings, child know,
God is wherever you go,
Shed a happy tear,
He is oh so near.

You Have No New Messages

2010

God checked His messages today,
He was amazed at what He heard.
Again, He didn't hear from you,
He heard nothing, not even a word.

You know that He loves you more,
Yet His love you continue to ignore.
He waits to hear from you each day,
But you still have nothing to say.

Once you surrender your fight,
Call Him in the morning or at night.
You suffer because you lost your light,
Call God, He will give you insight.

Do You Have a Minute?

2012

Do you have a minute or two? I know you're overwhelmed and exhausted. I know you work hard and often feel unappreciated. I know you're busy. I was just wondering if you had a minute or two? Can you stop? Are you still with Me? I'm still with you.

Do you have a minute or two? I won't stop you for too long. You've got so much to do. I see you. You're busy, I know, I understand. I see your every smile and your every tear. I love you.

Do you have a minute or two? I just wanted you to know it's going to be okay. That never-ending problem you have is going to go away. I see you struggle to make yourself and everyone you love happy, but somehow you fall short of your goal. It's okay. I love you. I hear you.

Do you have a minute or two? I have a wish. My wish is, for you to think of Me. My dear child, I think of you every moment of your day. I watch you grow and change. I love you so much. I know your pain and I know your joy.

68

Do you have a minute or two? I'll repeat my request. My wish is, that you think of Me. My wish is that you love Me like I love you. My wish is that you love each other. My wish is that you help each other and help yourself with My love. Are you still with Me? I'm still with you. I see you and I hear you, I love you so much.

Do you have a minute or two? My wish is that you share My love and My wish with everyone you know and everyone you don't know. I love you so and I believe in you. Do you believe in Me? . . . Thank you.

Love,

Jesus

Dancing With God

2009

We were poetry in motion,
We were rhythm of the ocean.
We were Ginger Rogers and Fred Astaire,
When I danced with God nothing could compare.

Our steps were a peaceful, smooth waltz,
Love and joy were our pulse.
I smiled with my happy heart,
I promised God, "We'll never part."
The memory of our dance is divine,
God said, "You're a sweet child of Mine."

When I danced with God, I walked on air,
When I danced with God, life I could bare.
When I danced with God, my spirit would soar,
When I danced with God, I had pain no more.

. . . Then the devil cut in with his tempting grin,
And I didn't think twice about his price.
The devil said, "You only live once, God's such a bore."
The devil insisted, "Dance with me, we'll tear up the floor."

Like a fool, I let go of God's hand,
Like a fool, I danced in the devil's band.
The cruel devil lied, and on my feet he stepped.
I didn't like his dance, inside I wept.

The devil called me names; he threw my heart on the floor,
He yelled, "DANCE FOOL, YOU WANT TO DANCE!"
But I could dance no more.

Then he said, "Drink fool, have a drink, you'll be able to dance."
He said, "Have nine, you'll feel fine, you'll be in a happy trance."
So I partied with the devil 'til I stumbled around,
I partied with the devil until I fell down.

…And he kicked me. And he kicked me. And he kicked me again.
He yelled, "FOOL YOU WANT SOME MORE!?
'Else get off my dance floor."
I cried hard as I crawled away,
I made a wrong choice, and I had to pray.

As I cried out, "God, God, help me please,"
The cold dance floor hurt my knees.
I cried, "God, I've had enough, I don't want to dance here.
Forgive me God; it's You I want near."

God answered, "Child of mine, don't say another word,
I still love you My child, your prayers are heard."
So again I danced with God in the light,
God said, "I'll always love you My child,"
He held me tight, and then, I was alright.

Got God

1981

You used to ignore me,
And I thought I was gonna die.
You used to say mean things,
Words that made me cry.

You used to put me down,
And stomp my heart on the ground.
And I used to stay there.

I used to stay there,
And look at my pain.
I used to blame me,
I used to go insane.

I used to feed my sadness,
I used to forget my gladness.
I used to stay in madness,
I used to be a bad mess.

Now I see it wasn't about me,
It's true; you know not what you do.
I understand you don't have a clue,
It's not about me, it's about you.

Poor me used to play that,
Poor me used to be a door mat.
Now I don't play,
Now I got somethin' to say.
I don't believe your lies,
I got wise.

I got God on my team,
I know life is but a dream.
I got a new show,
I don't play that no mo.

A Soldier's Heart

2014

It was day break in an old war, another battle and an endless challenge. Slowly the young soldier moved into position. He wished the war was over. He wanted to go home. He was sick of fighting; and sick of the smells, sounds, and sights of war.

Within minutes a bullet from an enemy gun blasted the soldier's right hand. It wasn't the first bullet to scar his young body. Like scorching lava burning a hole through his hand, the pain was intense.

The teenage soldier looked to Heaven. He didn't cry and he didn't ask why. He prayed,

"Jesus help me." With his left hand he applied pressure to his wound.

The soldier was distraught, and thought (*un-soldier*) thoughts. His pain became madness. He was mad from watching his friends suffer and die. He was mad at the war. He was even mad at Jesus.

The sky became dark as the despondent soldier voiced his rage. He stood and yelled to Heaven, "Jesus I'm in pain. I'm tired. I can't do this!" Suddenly a bright light devoured the dark sky. Then right before the young soldier's fiery eyes, Jesus appeared.

"Oh my Jesus," the soldier cried, as he fell to his knees. Jesus listened as the broken soldier continued. He said, "Jesus I can't do this." Jesus touched the young man's head, "My son you can do the job you were born to do."

The soldier stood up and revealed his wound to Jesus. He said, "Look what they did to me." Calmly Jesus showed the soldier the palms of His hands.

Tears rolled down the young soldier's dirty face. He apologized, "I'm sorry Jesus. I'm your soldier, I work for you." He cried, "No one will believe me."

Jesus hugged the young man and said, "I love you. I believe you."

It's Not too Late

2014

"You will never be happy! It's too late. It's too late for you!" Satan yelled at me.

I was silent. I thought, "I'm no fool. I'd be a fool to believe that. Even if I die tomorrow, it's not too late for me."

It's only too late if you don't believe
It's only too late if your life you grieve
It's only too late if your heart is stone
It's only too late if you think you're alone
It's only too late if you block God's love
It's only too late if you don't rise above

Rise above your hurt and your pain
Rise above the storm and the rain
Rise above your emotional spin
Then pray and let God in

It's not too late to surrender the fight
It's not too late to embrace the light
It's not too late to open your eyes
It's not too late to stop believing lies
It's not too late for the blind to see
It's not too late for you and for me.

Who's the Man?

2014

Long ago, but not so far away, in the land of surrender lived a gentle wise man. A lost and confused young woman stumbled through his gate and onto his property. Broken-hearted she was searching for work and a new life. In the beautiful country, with towering green trees and happy birds, the wise man showed her his home.

She noticed people working. Unique, colorful people of all ages were busy working with a smile. The young woman marveled at the contagious loving vibration that blessed her. The wise man introduced her to everyone.

She absorbed the peace and savored the love that radiated through this gracious man's house. But she wondered, "How is there enough work? How does everyone get along? And why do they love working for this man?" Many questions floated through her mercurial mind as she walked with the wise man.

"This is your place," he smiled as he showed her a quaint room with an arch shaped window. She loved her room. She beamed, "Thank you, it's perfect." He replied, "Thank you; we need devoted people for our work." He continued, "People come and people go. They come for happiness and a new life, but often they leave."

"My child," he smiled, "Straight is the difficult way and narrow is my gate. There are few who find it and few that stay." She asked, "Do they ever come back?" He answered, "Absolutely. People return when they realize they do in fact have a heart for this work. Many get to know and love me, so they stay forever." Then he touched her shoulder and asked, "Will you be staying?"

His question took her by surprise and pierced her heart. She took a deep breath and answered, "I hope so." "Good," his wise eyes lit up. "Hope is good."

The young woman loved spending time with him and she enjoyed the lessons the wise man taught. She learned so much at the land of surrender. But she is human. She left this haven and returned numerous times throughout her life.

Twenty years later, once again, she passed through his gate onto his magnificent property. The welcoming trees and birds greeted her. The old friends she made still lived there and were still smiling. They silently embraced her. They were happy to see her again.

Tears filled her old eyes and once more she knocked on his door. The tears rolled down her cheeks as he opened the door. He smiled and she smiled. He hugged her. "It's good to see you. I had faith in you. I knew you'd come home," he said.

"I'm sorry I left you," she cried. He consoled her, "You're forgiven. You mustn't be so hard on yourself. My love is unconditional."

As they walked, he stopped and gently put his hand on her shoulder and asked, "Will you be staying?" With confidence and the unleashed spirit of a brave heart she answered, "Yes!"

Wrong Train

2014

She was lost in the wilderness, it's true,
Her train derailed, but no one knew.
Numb, with a heart of stone,
Like a Zombie, she walked alone.

It was pouring rain, but she didn't care.
Her mind was blown, she wasn't aware.
She was out of prayers and out of tears,
She wandered for days or was it years?

Suddenly Jesus took her hand.
He said, "This isn't what God planned."
He picked her heart up off the ground,
She was lost, but now she's found.

Jesus told her, "Life isn't something to dread.
Life is to be living, not walking dead."
She cried, "What do I do?"
Jesus said, "Forgive and stop feeling sorry for you."

Jesus continued, "You lost your grip,
You had a bad trip.
With too much pain on your brain,
You boarded the wrong thoughts train."

He preached, "Take a deep breath and say,
Whenever I'm lost, I will be okay.
I will surrender the fight.
I'm always in God's sight."

He smiled, "The wilderness made you strong,
Now go and help others that think wrong.
My child, if you think the light way,
There is hope for a better day."

Freedom

2011

Freedom is a hummingbird
She sometimes speaks a humming word
She flies best wearing her bullet proof vest
She sports headphones playing her favorite song
Freedom can fly; oh watch her fly, all day long

Freedom has places to go and people to see
She will teach you to fly, she even taught me
She told me her secret; she said, "Face your fear,
You can fly in the dark; trust God's light is near."
Freedom hummed, "Remember me, and remember my tiny heart,
When you fly I'm by your side, we will never part."

Life's Tough Stuff

2015

"Like fish need water, you need Me," God said. "When a fish leaves water, the fish struggles for life. When water is poured on the fish, it has a brief relief. Fish need to be submerged in water like you need to be submerged in Me."

The Lord continued, "When you stay with Me and pray to Me you do well. With hope, trust, and love, you faithfully swim through life's tough stuff like a carefree happy fish."

God explained, "When you leave Me, like a fish without water you gasp for air. You drown in life's tough stuff and make wrong choices to numb your pain. If you do not return to Me and My unconditional love, you self-destruct and perish."

God smiled, "A fish in a little water swims okay for a day. Fish need plenty of water to thrive, dive, and to stay alive. So when you sink, and the water is over your head from life's tough stuff, swim to Me, I'll save you."

Section Three
My Mother's Love

Cynthia Santiago

Starts With Love

1979

For my mother, Dolores

Who's smarter than me because you've lived longer? You are.
Who picked up the pieces from many a hurt? You have.
Who for years was there to listen and teach? You were.
Who guided, cried, laughed and worried? You did.

Who foresaw my future -- if only I'd listened? My Mom.
Who warned, "Wherever you run, you take you?" My Mom.
Who let me learn the hard way, the only way I could? My Mom.
Who taught me time heals, but healing is slow? My Mom.

Who named me at birth -- Cynthia Lynne? My Mother.
Who gifted me with inner beauty, only I can thank? My Mother.
Who taught me God is the way through darkness and fear? My
Mother.
Whose patience was tried time and again? My Mother's.

What comes from Dolores, Mother and Mom? Your love.
What's more beautiful than a sunset on a summer day? Your love.
What's as precious as my daughter is to me? Your love.
What's shown me forgiveness, strength and truth? Your love.

Who will love you when nobody else does?
God, your mother, and your daughter.

Starts with love; ends with love.

A Lonely Train Ride

1989

I am riding on a southbound train to San Diego from Buena Park, CA. I relax in my window seat. The penetrating train whistle cries out to the night. Like a fire-breathing dragon, the powerful train demands respect. My ears pop as I watch the city lights swiftly pass by. My suitcase occupies the seat next to me. I avoid eye contact with people still searching for a place to sit.

It feels like I'm on a carnival ride. My seat faces north while the train rapidly rolls south. I take a deep breath and see my reflection in the window. Nobody on this car is talking. Maybe they're like me, all talked out.

This is a first. I'm traveling without my daughters. I'm on my way home from spending 24 hours with my mother. Today is her 54th birthday. I think we talked non-stop for 18 hours. I enjoyed our quality time together. I wonder why it took me 11 years to make this two-hour trip alone? It's probably because I'm a mother first and a daughter second. I get pulled between the females I love.

My eyes are tired and my throat is sore. Last night we talked and she smoked 'til after 1 a.m. I figured I'd sleep on the train-ride home. Instead I think of her . . . and I think of us.

We celebrated her birthday with lunch at a restaurant we've been to before, once for my birthday and once for her mother's (my Nana). At lunch we talked as if we were trying to beat the clock. We didn't waste a moment of our precious time. I miss my mother, but not as much as I'll miss her someday.

She's changed in the last few years since her mother died. I don't know exactly how she's changed, but she's different. Along with being thinner and older, she's wiser. She's wiser, yet still learning. I suppose it's an ongoing test, learning to live without a mother you love dearly.

My mother's more serious now. Sure, we laugh and joke. I can always make her laugh. But sometimes there's pain on her face because there's pain in her heart. My mother had a happy birthday today, but no day, especially birthdays, come without memories of her mother. My Nana and my mother were very close. But Nana is gone and with her is part of my mother's heart.

I'm scared to walk where my mother has walked. I can't imagine life without her. Christmas and my birthday and her birthday and . . . when I dial her phone number she just has to answer.

When I'm 54-years-old I will sit across my birthday cake and look into the loving eyes of my dear 72-year-old mother. She'll be there . . . you see, I can't live with half a heart.

She was there, we celebrated together ... and then, three months later, she was gone.

If I Could Howl

1992

If I could howl like a wild animal I would. Since I can't, I will do the next best thing, write … with Niagara tears gushing from my eyes I can't see what I'm writing. I nervously dig my thumbnail into my forefinger. I think of my mother's tears and our sad good-bye.

The road is bumpy, words jump off the line. Our white truck is packed to the top of its shell. I look in the mirror to see my brother, Donnie, behind us. His truck is also loaded down.

We're on our way home from Buena Park, CA to San Diego. It's Sunday afternoon and everyone in the truck is quiet. My mother's voice echoes in my head, and I cry.

We hugged like there is no tomorrow. We sobbed and we couldn't let go. She cried, "Why does it seem like we're always saying good-bye?"

With a truck load of furniture and things from mom, my heart breaks because I'll never pass this way again. As we approach the 405 freeway I glance again and see Donnie behind us. I pray our trip home is safe.

It's 2 o'clock and the sun is scorching my face. My eyes are swollen and tired. There's a lot of traffic. My stomach aches and like a child, I miss my mother.

Due to circumstances beyond her control, after living almost 20 years in Buena Park, CA my mother is moving to her mountain home in Big Bear, CA. Though she'll only be another hour away, the move makes me very uncomfortable.

My mother generously gave Donnie and me many nice things that won't fit in her Big Bear cabin. It feels strange having her special belongings while she's alive. It's been an emotional weekend.

With every barrel and every box we carried out, mom cried. She said, "Part of me is going to your house and part of me is going to Donnie's."

My mother is getting older and I haven't accepted the fact that I'll lose her someday. She's changed since losing her mother. Undoubtedly I won't be the same without her.

Donnie just passed us. I noticed Mom's granny square afghan on his front seat. I wonder what he is thinking? His truck is all tied up like the Beverly Hillbillies.

Last night we slept on the floor in sleeping bags. This morning we fished in an ice chest for sodas. After we ate stale Imperial Beach donuts for breakfast, we walked to the park.

While Misty (my nine-year-old) yelled, "Push me!" from the merry-go-round, Mom and I sat on the park bench and talked. It's a tragedy and it hurts that my mother is so unhappy.

The sun has moved, my little brother is behind us and the sign says San Diego 64 miles. We're halfway home . . . I've stopped crying.

Somehow the *light* is back in my face. I see the ocean, the beautiful, blue ocean. I think of mom, train rides and long distance phone calls. The sign says San Diego 44 miles. I can't wait to get home to call her and say, "I love you, thanks for everything. I miss you."

As we passed through Oceanside I stopped writing to rest for a while, Donnie is in front of us and the sign says San Diego 35 miles. I feel better, we're getting closer. It was a long ride, but it went fast. Like life.

Carlsbad next seven exits and the Temptations are singing, "I wish it would rain." It's a miracle my kids are still quiet. No wonder, Brandy (my 14-year-old), is sleeping and Misty is eating candy.

It's just me and my thoughts drifting down I-5. Fairgrounds next exit means, "Home sweet home." There it is, "San Diego City Limits". . .

With my faithful husband, Jr., at the wheel, this two hour trip comes to an end and I close yet another chapter in the story of my mother's life . . . Chula Vista 23 miles.

The Way We Were

2000

"And when one of us is gone and one of us is left to carry on, then remembering will have to do, our memories alone will get us through, you and me against the world."
-Helen Reddy early '70s.

My Dearest Mother,

I remember when you dedicated that song to us, and you also insisted, "Have you never been mellow," by Olivia Newton-John, was written for me.

I recall the trials and tribulations of the early '70s. I was a teenager and you were in your thirties. Often, instead of you and me against the world, it was you and me against each other. Like Barbara Streisand sang, "Misty water colored memories of the way we were."

In the '70s you were beautiful. Everyone thought you were pretty and everyone noticed your tanned, shapely legs. I was jealous. I'd look at my short, white legs and they certainly didn't look like your long legs. How else does a teenage girl feel when she's cursed with her father's legs? Luckily I outgrew that stage.

During the '70s I was a mixed up confused (definitely not mellow) young woman growing up too fast. I was leather, I was lace. I was up, I was down. I lived on sunflower seeds and the beach. I was tan, blonde, childfree, wrinkle free, and living in the fast lane.

I'm thankful I survived. I'm grateful time and time again God reminded me to slow down, and to, "Be still." God helped me to stay when I'd pray. And God taught me, "This too shall pass." You also reminded me of those things. You reminded me to make the right choice. You were a serious mother, but you were a fun mother. You said what you meant and meant what you said. When you caught me making bad choices I paid a price. You tried to hammer in my airhead, "Something you do in one minute can change your life."

One of my best lessons was being 16 and wanting a "to die for" black, polka dot bikini. It was on sale. I tried it on and (to my dismay) you said, "Not a chance!" We argued. Rather, I argued, to no avail. The answer was, NO! (You made me sick) I looked dynamite in it. So I stole it. And that was that.

90

After you left the dressing room I put my 27x30 Levis over the darling bikini bottom and my T-shirt over the adorable bikini top. I was a nervous wreck but I thought you were none the wiser. You'd never know. I'd only wear it to the beach or to my best friend, Mickie's pool. I had to have it.

After a quiet ride home, I flew to my room to quickly strip the bikini off and hide it in a drawer. You barged in like Sergeant Carter. As I stood (caught with my pants down) you scolded, "I'll take that!" I could have died.

You blew my mind. You didn't lecture me or hit me. You were weird, quite mysterious. You didn't say anything. I wondered what you were up to. Maybe you were going to drag me back to the store to return it.

The following weekend I *had a heart attack*. There you were bigger than all outdoors looking like a beachy, cool, Annette Funicello or a young Liz Taylor. You were Coppertone covered, lying on your lawn chair, with a cold one, wearing MY BIKINI! Then you smirked, "It is kinda cute isn't it?" I pleaded my case that it wasn't fair. You ignored me and lit a cigarette.

You wore my bikini all summer. I never forgot and I didn't find it amusing.

Oh the '70s. We fought and we talked. We spent a lot of time at the beach and the drive-in movies. You chaperoned my many slumber parties. We shared tears and we shared laughter.

I can't believe some of the capers we pulled off. A woman with your morals and good common sense actually snuck teenage girls into the drive-in. We hid in the trunk of your car. We had a blast.

You drove your notorious '69, brown Thunderbird with a trunk load of teenage girls. You drove in like you knew what you were doing. After a few minutes you opened the trunk (like a pro) and out we crawled. You were 'bitchin. (Except for the bikini episode.)

Summer's meant fun. We had fun in the sun. And summer meant slumber parties. Twenty girls slept outside in our backyard in sleeping bags. One birthday bash, you, Ms. Sherlock Holmes, popped outside (without warning) for a head count. You noticed Terry was missing. You gave us five minutes to produce her (fat chance with no cell phones). It seems like yesterday, I can still see you dialing her mother when she walked into your bedroom with her big blue eyes. (Whew!)

There were many other slumber parties. One night there was a hidden six pack of beer in the bushes. Since no one would claim it you opened a can and said, "Thanks girls." (Brat.)

I remember you. You always looked and smelled good (Thanks to Estee Lauder.) How did you always look good? Your hair and make-up was flawless. Your fingernails and toenails painted. Everybody liked you, you were the cool mom.

During my teenage years, what other catastrophes did I get myself into? Oh, how about the night I said I was going to Mar Vista pool (where I was allowed) but instead I went to the Mar Vista High School dance which was forbidden.

Well, Mic and I wanted to go and everybody else was going. Geez, she lived right across the street from the school. Heck, we could walk to the dance. So we said we were going to the pool. Since I was spending the night with Mic, it was simple.

I was wrong again. After the dance at 11:30 p.m., walking to Mic's house, I spotted your dastardly T-bird. My heart dropped. "Oh my God, I'm dead, my mother's here!" I freaked. I thought about going the other way.

We walked in and your face was not happy. "Get your things Cynthia Lynne!" My heart raced, when I was Cynthia Lynne I was about to get killed. Mic and I fumbled around in her room looking for my stuff. We were silent.

How about the time you and dad went out and Mic spent the night. I had the brilliant idea to have an egg fight. It was glorious. In the bathroom we sported shower caps and bikinis. Then on the word, "GO!" we went crazy egging each other until a dozen eggs were smashed into some funny places. We laughed hysterically. (I miss Mic, God bless her pretty soul in Heaven.)

After our mischievous mess we took showers and cleaned up. The bathroom stunk like eggs. It was gross. No problem, we cleaned like there was no tomorrow. We cleaned and laughed. We cleaned the walls, the floor, and we shook the rugs. We cleaned the sink, the tub, anywhere and everywhere. It was perfect. We sprayed room deodorizer so there was no sign of fun. No evidence. We were good. (We weren't that good.)

The next morning, Mic and I ate your homemade chocolate cake for breakfast. We sat at the kitchen table while you sat down with your coffee. (You had that "Cynthia Lynne" look on your face.) Then you jolted us, "Girls do you want to tell me about the egg fight in the bathroom last night?" We about fainted. How'd you know? You escorted us to the bathroom and pointed to the ceiling. (Whoops!)

Mom, there are so many memories of my teenage years. This is a mere chapter from our book. It seems like my teenage years almost killed us.

Now that I'm a mother, I realize you were trying to protect me. You stayed on my heels because you loved me. It wasn't that you were mean or unreasonable, it's just that you cared and you worried.

Like the time I said I was going to the movies. Instead, I went to an un-chaperoned pool party. I was told not to go. I went anyway. Boy did I pay a price.

Wouldn't you know it, just my luck; someone shut the sliding glass door right before I ran through it. BOOM! OUCH! I can still see the look on your face. My friends had me in the bathroom with wash cloths on wounds, applying pressure to stop blood. When I heard, "Your mother's here!" I wanted to disappear.

Your face was pale. You were silent. It seemed like forever. Then I pleaded, "Say something, please say something." You preached, "You are lucky to have all your limbs."

That night at the hospital I lay in a bloodstained bikini while I was stitched from top to bottom. I had a bad injury on my back, plus my legs, my face, and a wicked one on my wrist. I have the ugly scars. I just wanted to have fun.

Mom, remember the fun we had every summer at Silver Strand Beach? How about the time you took a bunch of girls and we rented rafts? We were out on the water having a great time when we spotted some deranged woman waving her arms furiously doing some kind of emergency gesture. Oh gee, it was you in your sun hat, shades and smock. Yikes, we drifted north, almost to the next town (dang current). We went to shore and walked the mile back to you. Sorry mom.

It was an adventure and it was never a dull moment. From catching me ditching school, "How was school today Cynthia Lynne?" To catching me flipping you off as I walked down the hall. (I was cool).

Yeah right, I was cool until you flew down the hall and hit me like a ton of bricks. I forgot the kitchen wall was mirrors. I was dumb and you were quick.

I'll close with, "Thank you mom. Thanks for putting up with me during my teenage years. And, "Hey, if you happen to see the most beautiful girl in the world, won't you tell her that I love her."

Happy Mother's Day

2003

"Happy Mother's Day," from my little corner of the world. Like Forrest Gump said, "Life is like a box of chocolates, you never know what you're gonna get."

* * *

My Dear Mother,

I enjoyed our recent weekend at your beautiful Big Bear home. Thank you so much for your hospitality.

I love spending time with you. My favorite memory of us was laughing at the movies. Sitting next to you watching, "Anger Management" was so much fun. We laughed like we didn't have a care in the world. It was priceless.

Just like last summer, we sat together and cried when we watched the Disney movie, "Spirit." It was a good movie too, huh mom?

Mother, I love going to the movies with you. Since I can remember we've been going to the movies and pigging out on salty, buttered popcorn.

We've seen so many movies together. Through the years we've laughed and cried. From "Imitation of Life" to "Terms of Endearment", oh don't forget "Beaches" and "Bambi." There are too many movies to remember, too many movies to list. I love all our times together.

As usual, I felt better and saner after spending time with you. Thank you for being my friend, my advisor, and my confidant. You always make me feel important.

Spending time with you was comforting like when I was a little girl and I sat on your lap; you wiped my tears and calmed my fears.

Right now it's raining outside. The house is quiet: everyone's asleep. I stopped writing to check my old dog, "Friday." Thanks mom for being concerned when "Friday" was in the hospital.

Mother, you are a blessing. I think of you more than you know. Every creative thing I attempt, I think, "Mom would do it this way." Like the other night I brought home a beautiful bouquet of flowers, and I thought of you when I arranged them. You're a natural with flowers.

Do you remember when I was a little girl and you worked arranging feather flowers at Marvell's Flower Shop on Palm Avenue? I think you were in your twenties and you wore Avon's, Topaz perfume. It seems like yesterday, not forty years ago.

Mom, do you remember when I was little and we colored together? One of my favorite things was coloring in my color book, with you coloring the page next to mine. You colored better than me, yet you made my page seem like a masterpiece. I loved our time playing together when I was small.

To this day, when I smell Play-Doh, I think of us making clay creations. The aroma of a fresh can of Play-Doh brings back fond mommy-and-daughter memories.

Where does the time go? Mom, we have so much to be thankful for, and I'm grateful you recovered from the mini-stroke you had a year ago. It was more than challenging to be with you when you weren't healthy. I was overcome with fear and numb beyond words when you weren't you. I never thought I would get you back. I just wanted more time.

Seeing you weak, when you have always been strong, horrified me. I couldn't cope with you being sick, and I hated the thought of possibly losing you. I prayed and I prayed, and finally, my prayers were answered. You came back. Praise God, you came back from your long journey of mental confusion and physical restrictions.

In fact, you came back, and you regained your strength just in time to hold my hand and walk with me through my surgery and recovery. As long as I live I won't forget the look in your eyes that August day at the hospital when you had to let go of my hand. Hours later when I opened my eyes, there you were. And you said, "Hi Honey."

Thank you for taking such good care of me. Again you saved the day. Just like when your granddaughters were born. You were there to help me. I love you so much.

My angel night light glows with serenity, and I'm blessed you are healthy and we have more time together.

With you in Big Bear and me in Imperial Beach, we don't see enough of each other. We talk on the phone, but it's not like a walk-and-talk with us holding hands. It's not like you reading to me. I love when we sit on the bed and you read to me. I cherish those moments; you've read to me for almost fifty years.

Mother's Day and every day, remember I love you dearly, and I thank God for our many years together. Your faith, your determination, and your spirit is amazing.

Life truly is like a box of chocolates, and mother in my box of chocolates I'm grateful I got you.

Love Will Find a Way

2004

For My Mother Dolores

Mother it looks like you're sad today

Walking alone in a cloud so gray

In that cloud you can't find your way

Can't cope, so you hope, you even pray

Pressure and pain froze your brain

And life, mother, drives you insane

You fight that cloud, it won't go away

Fight with all your might, "Not fair," you say

97

You can't stand that cloud, it won't disappear
You're forever trapped, in the dark you fear
You hate the cloud, it won't let you go
It broke your heart and left your spirit low

So you walk through life with a sad face
And love, what's love, you can't embrace
You're dead inside and you can't hide
Your black cloud has you on a dark ride

Then you remembered what you once knew
All things are possible with God it's true
When you think of God, He thinks of you
God has the power to turn your black cloud blue

"You must stop hating the cloud," God said
Stop fighting and forgive. Try love instead
For when you fight you're fighting blind
Mom, let the cloud go and love you'll find

Her Last Mother's Day

2007

Dear Mother,

On this mother's day I want to remind you that it is my pleasure to be your guiding light during your most recent challenges and changes. I want you to know that your tears are my tears. Your fears are my fears. Your happiness is my happiness. Your smile is my strength. And your laughter is my spirit. I love when we laugh together.

God has a plan and though we don't understand, we must trust. Shoot, beats me how we get through this crazy life. Nobody knows what we endure and overcome, nobody knows but us and God, huh Mom?

I want to remind you that I see you when I'm not with you. I see you and I see us. I see our good times and our not so good times. And I always see our love.

I see you holding me last winter as I cried because I lost my best friend, "Friday." I lost my 18-year-old. She was so much more than a dog, she was my baby. When I cried, "I'm sorry mom that 'Friday' is buried on your birthday," you smiled and said, "Honey, it's an honor."

We take one step at a time, one day at a time. I am your guide. God guides me. We try to stay out of the dark and stay in the light. It isn't easy huh, mom? Seems like the dark just grabs us and we must continue to fight for the light. It's good to know the sun will always come out tomorrow. I love you. We will battle the storms together, pray and wait for the calm. Then we will embrace joy so we can live, love and laugh together.

I love when we laugh, especially at Hallmark when we open every single musical card and crack up. One time two ladies had a blast laughing with us. The one gal was cracking up so hard she said, "This card is so good I think I'll send it to someone I hate." Yeah, I love when we laugh.

Oh and I see you at Boll Weevil restaurant when we order our usual, mozzarella sticks and flaming hot chicken strips with extra everything. It's always finger lickin' good and, "More napkins please."

I also see you at Carrow's restaurant eating your favorite cinnamon French toast.

The day they brought it to you smothered in strawberries and whip cream you should have seen your face. Your eyes got real big and you said, "Heavenly."

And every time I say, "God bless this meal," you always say, "God bless this day." God bless you mother.

I see us sitting at the Coronado shore watching people and watching birds. Just walking and talking and watching the clouds. You mention the clouds and the color of the sky. You've taught me to notice the important things. And you always predict the rain right on schedule. How do you do that mom?

This is a good one. When you got your physical exam last month, right in the middle of the action, you asked the doctor, "Are we having fun yet?" That's where I get my sense of humor.

What else? Oh, I see you at bingo. Especially the night you hit me. (Child abuse.) Geez Louise, there you were hitting me on my arm like a lunatic and I complained "OW!" Then you showed me the $100 rip off ticket you won. You were speechless. Then we laughed. I love to laugh with you mom. I already said that.

Another time at bingo you tricked me. You knew something I didn't know. You told me you were on fire and just needed number 16. Okay, my heart raced as I glued my eyes to the spinner, watching for ball 16 to pop out. Instead ball 33 popped out and you yelled B I N G O, like you knew what you were doing.

Great, I was ready to climb under the table as you yelled bingo and waved your card. (Lord have mercy.) Then you leaned over in my ear and said, "I needed 33 too. Cynthia, you thought I made a mistake didn't you?" (Yup.)

I see you at C.V.S. when we were shopping, as usual, for the stuff on our list. Somehow we lost track of each other and I heard a piercing loud, "CYN-THEE-AH!" I whistled back and found you. It broke my heart that you were worried even for a moment. I love you.

I see you walking your precious poodle, "Missy." You both walk so proud. You and your "furry daughter" as you call her. She's lucky to have you. And you are blessed to have her devotion. Like "Friday," your companion, "Missy" is unconditional love.

One of my favorite memories is of you at my work picnic by the Coronado shore. It was nice you got to meet my second family. I can still hear the echo when you met my friends. They said, "We just love your daughter." You answered, "I love her too."

I see you smiling sitting in the lawn chair enjoying the sun and the beautiful view. At the end of the day you were pretty creative stacking the cooler on top of the stroller. One of my friends told me, "Your mom is an angel." I agree.

Before I forget, I want to thank you for your many prayers. Thank you so much mom for praying for my family and friends. I appreciate it.

There is so much I could write and have written about through the years. I must add the vision of you in Wal-Mart with your "buggy" as you call it. I see you loading up all kinds of chocolate. I said, "Mom that's a lot of chocolate." You looked at me with your serious face and said, "Didn't you hear, chocolate is good for you?"

Well, I am past deadline, the story of my life. What do you say, "A day late and a dollar short?" I could write more but will close with "Happy Mother's Day I'm glad we're together." And quit repeating that you don't need anything. I know, I know.

I will tell you again, "I love you mom, God knows I love you so much and I'm blessed you are here. Like the '70's song, "You and me Against the World."

Bingo

2007

I woke at 3 a.m. again. It's been that way for a while. At midnight, my husband, Jr. asked, "Cin, Cin are you okay?" I was gazing into space. I answered, "I'm thinking about my mother."

My mother has pancreatic cancer. The same disease that took her mother's life. My mother took care of my Nana for the last year of her life. Indeed, "Terms of Endearment." My nana passed away on December 12, 1984. After many prayers, while holding Nana's hand, my mother sang, "The Twelve Days of Christmas" to Nana over and over again until Nana left her body.

Mother and I went to bingo again tonight. It has been our Wednesday night ritual for the past couple of years. My mother had intense pain this morning. I was out of my mind worrying. I quickly gave her morphine. Guiding her on this journey isn't something I thought I could do. By the grace of God, I am doing it.

Anyway, I watched my mother take care of my Nana. I watched my Nana get thinner and weaker. As they traveled their journey together my mother was always in control. Nana had surgery, chemotherapy and radiation. Nana helped plan her own funeral, down to what she wore. I watched them through my tears. It's been two months since my mother's dreadful diagnosis. It was surreal to hear those unforgiving words, "It's stage four cancer. Surgery is not an option. The cancer has spread too far." Chemotherapy and radiation would not extend my mother's life. I was hysterical.

That dark day, Jr. asked the doctor questions and my mother was calm. She didn't act like someone had just told her something horrifying. In fact, she replied, "One thing I know for sure is, we're going to bingo tonight." We went to bingo that Wednesday night. The confusion in my head screamed. Nothing made sense. I was in an emotional spin. My tummy ached, my heart was broken, and there we were, at bingo. Mom is something else.

Only God knows when she will further this journey to Heaven and let go of my hand. Tonight at bingo her skin felt different. It felt cool. I kept asking her if she was cold and she said she was fine. I don't mean to mother her or smother her. She looked pale and tired. My mother's almost 72 year-old body was wearing out.

Mother enjoyed bingo tonight. She loves seeing her friends and family. Her sister, my Aunt Karen and Uncle Bob are here from Iowa. My brain keeps reminding me of what my heart doesn't want to remember. When I look in my Aunt Karen's eyes I see my pain.

Mother is sleeping more and eating less. Her pain is increasing but it doesn't stop her. Her sense of humor is great. Her spirits are high. She is such a soldier. She does not feel sorry for herself. She tells me, "I'll be strong enough for both of us. It's better me than you." She says, "It's God's will. Honey, it's in God's plan."

Hospice is on board. God bless the Hospice angels. Dr. Sylvia, Nurse Sara and miracle worker, Christina are truly angels. And Chaplin Ron, he is God sent. Thank you all for making a difference on my mother's journey. My mother adores you and looks forward to seeing you. She calls you her "Welcome Committee." In fact she told me to remember you at Christmas if she is not here.

It's 5a.m., I've made a collage with dozens of pictures of my precious mother. Her smile is radiant. It's bizarre to think of her being away one day. But the truth is comforting. The truth is, when she leaves her diseased body she will be born again in Heaven. God doesn't lie.

My mother is an angel and will always be an angel. When my mother arrives, she will get to see those she has missed. The good Lord will stand with her sweet Grandma Shannon and her parents; Nana and Poppy.

My birthday is this month. The only thing I want for my birthday is for my mother to be happy. She told me she'll be here. She smiled, "I'll be here to spank you."

Mother reminded me that it is Dena's (her great-grand baby's) first birthday. Mother said, "Honey, the old leave to make room for the young."

I'd like to say, "Happy first birthday Dena, my little sweetheart. And Mother I will always love you."

That's the Way Love Goes

2007

I am losing my dear mother to pancreatic cancer. I am her care bear and her care giver. Unconditional love stretched beyond my wildest dreams and nightmares. I am watching my mother slowly disappear.

Little did I know when God gave me this responsibility what an emotional roller coaster I would ride. Little did I know what a humbling experience I will remember the rest of my life. I watch her body fade away right before my tearful eyes.

Surrounded by love and the grace of God, my frail mother sat with us for Thanksgiving. Of course we made her a small plate. It smelled good to her. It was her traditional turkey and sage dressing recipe. She couldn't eat. It was heartbreaking. But she tried.

Words cannot express my joy in seeing her strong spirit. She is brave and has the determination of an Olympic athlete. My mother's will to live surpasses my understanding of what a body can endure. As I write and she sleeps, her weight is less than 80 pounds. When she painstakingly steps on the scale, I sneak my big toe on the back of it so she thinks she still weighs 105lbs. She smiles and says, "That's not bad, huh honey?"

My mother is not eating and has not eaten anything since my birthday in mid-September. She sips ice water and Coke, and that's all folks. You have no idea what this does to me that she can no longer sip broth, or drink the Boost drinks, or even eat her favorite peanut butter toast. I don't know what sustains her, evidently God's will.

It puzzles me; I guess she is living on love. The hospice Chaplin asked her, "Dolores, what are you waiting for?" She smiled and said, "Jesus."

She is weak and frail and needs a lot of help. (She is skin on bones.) I try not to cry around her but sometimes she says things to me that just knock me out. KO'd by this tiny little bird. This morning she said (again), "Cynthia, sit down honey. Come sit down by me. You know I'm leaving soon and you must be strong. Honey you are the best in the west and remember I will always be with you, always. And someday when your book comes out I will see you smile."

While I write, I have played Janet Jackson's old song, "That's The Way Love Goes," about 100 times. I keep hitting play after it ends. Why? Well because I like it and I am waiting for someone in *Santiago's Sanitarium* to complain. No one has. Maybe they know I have completely lost my mind. It makes me smile to do something weird for a change. My life has been so serious since my precious mother's diagnosis in July.

As I listen to Janet, I came across "Sometimes." I wrote it for my mom in1988. (Jr. just walked by, gave me a kiss and sang, "That's The Way Love Goes," cool huh?)

I just checked my mom (in my bedroom) and she is still sleeping peacefully. Praise the Lord. As I re-entered the front room, I smiled and danced my way toward the computer. I was doing an Ellen Degeneres dance all the way back. I was dancing with God. I was being me. It's time to surrender her to God. "That's The Way Love Goes."

Sometimes…

Sometimes I wonder if it is wise to love my mother so dearly. Sometimes I think about her everything, mostly her love. Sometimes I laugh at us and long to laugh with her again. She calls me and my morning voice cracks; I pour my coffee and wake to her words. Sometimes she visits me and my world makes sense.

Sometimes we watch sad movies together. Sometimes we hug and kiss like there is no tomorrow. Sometimes she cooks my favorite food and sometimes I cook hers. Sometimes she sews for me and I am surprised again.

Sometimes we shop and hold hands. Sometimes she treats me to lunch and we have fun. Sometimes we go to the beach and wear funny hats. Sometimes she makes my day when no one else can. Sometimes I worry about her too much. Sometimes we wear nighties and pig out on homemade, buttered popcorn.

Sometimes we play our favorite songs LOUD and dance. Sometimes I rub her sore back. Sometimes she brushes my long hair and says, "You have this thick hair because of me. I kept it short when you were a little girl."

Sometimes she gives me things I could never give myself. Sometimes we take long road trips together and we talk about everybody. Sometimes I look at her and I see me. Sometimes she winds my Grandfather clock and I see her mother, my Nana. Sometimes she is unhappy and so am I. Sometimes I wish someday will never come.

Sometimes she is mad and I'm glad not at me. Sometimes we exercise together, most times we don't. Sometimes we go to church and pray and cry. Sometimes I miss her every day. Sometimes I dwell on losing her and know I will be lost without her.

Sometimes I wish I could buy her the best gift and pick her the prettiest flower to remind her again I love her more than words. Sometimes I am scared to walk where she has walked and to shed the tears she has shed.

Sometimes I write foolish lines at foolish times and burn dinner. Sometimes I wonder how my mother got so beautiful inside and out.

God bless you,

 I love you Mom

December 8, 2007 holding my hand she left for Heaven

The Road

2008

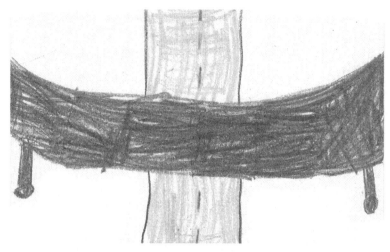

God helped me walk the roughest road of my life. A road that was dark and never-ending. A road I hated, fought and cried on . . . a road I almost died on . . . but because God helped me, and God loves me, I didn't stop. I continued to walk. I continued to talk. I continued to try, but often I'd sigh. So I walked slowly. And sometimes I crawled. And often I stalled. And when I wanted to quit God was there.

When I was blind, God helped me see. When I was numb, God helped me feel. When I was lost on that road, God helped me find my way. And when I was scared, and only God knew how very scared I was, God helped me feel safe so I could breathe again. God was always there and nothing can compare to His love.

God was there when I was out of control and made no sense. So again we talked and walked on the bumpy road with the barbwire fence . . . God helped me so I could continue to carry her.

Yes, I carried my precious mother, Dolores to her new home in Heaven. Yes, I carried her up the mountain and over the bridge. With God by my side I couldn't hide. So I cried, and cried and cried.

My pain was insane and my tears were like rain. On that road I slipped and fell, I wasn't very well. And God helped me again. Thank you. I love you. I will never forget that road and I will never forget God's love.

Cynthia Santiago

Good Enough for God

2009

God brought me here a long time ago,

He put me on earth to be in His show.

It was just me and my mommy when I was small,

Then it was me and my mom as I grew tall.

When I was a woman it was my mother and me,

God had a plan for us you see.

Sometimes we thought we weren't good enough

as we walked the mile,

When we thought we weren't good enough

we couldn't smile.

We loved each other as we walked and talked,

With God as our guide we had hope inside.

We'd get back up after a fall,

We held hands then gave God a call.

We cried, "We're not good enough, we can't win the race."

"We're not good enough we keep falling on our face."

God said, "Some throw stones and stones hurt it's true,

They judged My Son and yes, they judge you.

They judge all My children because they don't know,

I'll be watching when they reap what they sow."

God said, "You're good enough for Me, I made you this way,

Just be you, don't hear what they say."

So mother and me we shouted out loud,

"We're good enough for God! We're so proud."

God said, "My child, remember, don't hear what they say,

I decide who's good enough on judgment day."

God said, "Good enough, good enough for who?

Believe you're good enough for Me, I'll always love you. . ."

You Will See Me

11-16-10 would be her 75th birthday

Cynthia, you will see me when
You stop to see,
Everywhere you look
You will always see me.

You will see me at the beach,
You will see me in your car.
You will see me when
You look up at night,
I'm your shining star.
You will see me when
You wear my clothes,
You will see me when
You paint your toes.
You will see me when
You clear your throat,

111

You will see me when
You buy a new tote.
Yes, you will see me.

You will see me time and time again,
Because I'm more than your mother,
I am forever your friend.
You will see me in a crowd,
You will see me when you're proud.

You will see me at the mall,
You will see me in your hall.
You will see me when you cook,
You will see me when
You write your book.

Yes, you will see me
You will see me at the store,
You will see me say,
"I love you more."

You will see me when
You stop to pray,
You will see me
Every Mother's Day.

You will see me when
You watch the rain,
You will see me in
. . .unspoken pain.

You will see me when
You smell a rose.
You will see me when

No one knows.

You will see me when
You brush your teeth.
You will see me when
You hang my wreath.

Yes, you will see me.
Cynthia, you will see me when
You look in your mirror.
You will see me in your eyes
Daughter dear.

Silent Night, Holy Night

December, 2010

Three years ago, the moment my mother's heart stopped beating here and started beating in Heaven . . . she lost her battle with pancreatic cancer.

Did I really walk her across the bridge from here to there? Did I really hold her frail hand every step of the way? Yes I did. With tears rolling down my cheeks while trying to type through them, I realize I did it, wow, I really did it! Now, wiping tears off my lips, the lips she kissed day in and day out, while telling me, "Honey, you mustn't cry, honey you must be strong."

I couldn't stop crying. I cried a lot as I hugged her tiny body that worked so hard to live. I kissed her bony forehead and I wondered how I could exist without her. How could I exist without this precious, priceless woman? She was my mother, my mom, my mommy, and my friend. She was a friend who knew everything about me. She was a friend who gave me more than anyone will ever know. She gave me gifts from the heart. The gifts I give to my girls and anyone I love.

As I pause, reflect, and wipe my tears, the exact moment I woke this morning at 4 a.m., was the same time I woke three years ago while holding her hand. December 8, 2007, her heart, her lungs and her body stopped. She left her body. But she lives. Praise be to God. She lives, just not here.

Dolores J. is alive and well in Heaven. My mother is not and never will be dead. She is in my every day and my nights. She is light in my darkness. She is sunshine in my gloomy day. She is the love that gave me birth.

Only my mother and I were there when I was born. And yes, in God's miraculous plan, only she and I were there when she left my bedroom for Heaven. Her body was warm, and with her hand in mine, at that very moment, she slept in Heavenly peace.

I didn't know what to do when the hours on December 7, 2007 climbed towards midnight. With sweet hospice nurse, Brenda Jackson nearby, I began singing to mom. I sang Silent Night. I prayed every prayer I knew, for hours. I looked at my dear mother, knowing at any time she would leave, so I decided to sing Silent Night. I sang, "Silent night, holy night, all is calm all is right." I sang it over and over again. "Sleep in heavenly peace. *Sleeeep* in *Heavenlee* peace. *Siiiilent* night, *holee* night, all is calm, all is right, round young Virgin, Mother and child, holy infant so tender and mild."

Then I paused and asked Brenda, "When is she going to go?" Brenda, with her soft, dark-chocolate skin and loving brown eyes told me, "She will go once you fall asleep. She wants to trick you like Santa Claus."

I thought, "Then I will stay awake." Around 3a.m. my husband, Jr. checked us and gave mom another kiss. I held mom's left hand with half of me on my bed, the other half on the hospital bed with mom. Brenda was in a chair holding mom's right hand. I didn't tell Jr. what Brenda said. I just watched mom in her favorite pink sweater. I felt her feet, tucked her in to keep her warm, and kept singing Silent Night.

When my mother was with her mother (on the last night of my Nana's life) my mother sang the Twelve Days of Christmas to Nana. My Nana lost her battle with pancreatic cancer on December 12th, 1984. Unbelievable, huh?

Anyway, early the morning of December 8th, I closed my eyes for a minute. My hand was still in hers. That morning I fell asleep for a minute, just a tiny minute.

I opened my eyes around 4a.m. I looked at Mom. She looked the same but her chest was not moving up and down. I looked at Brenda with tears rolling down my cheeks. I cried, "Brenda, oh Brenda." She shook her head, "Yes." She said, "Yes, honey, Ms. Dolores went to Heaven."

I hugged my mother and cried. I sobbed, "I don't know what to do now. Oh God how can I go on? How can I do this?" Brenda said, "You will."

My mother looked so peaceful. I kept hearing her voice say, "Hon-nee don't do this to yourself. Cynthia you've got to be strong."

I took a deep breath and noticed through tears it was 5:15a.m. I wiped my nose and blew my nose. (I can't see the keys to type. Okay, I know where we were and where we are.)

My mother is fine. She is happy. She is my guardian angel. I have learned more since that December night and the following morning than I have learned in 50 years. We learn to walk. We stumble and fall but we walk again. Then we run, and even skip when we are happy, in tune with God...

Keep my mother alive by telling her story. Talk about us. Reflect on love and remember "All things are possible with God."

To Heaven

2012

Mother remember no matter how far,
I'll always love you, wherever you are.
Every day of my life I think of you,
And I'll dream of us 'til my dreams come true.

Mother I miss you painfully today,
Only memories, you've gone away.
Since you're an angel this Mother's Day,
To Heaven I'll send my love your way.

Cynthia Santiago

When Now is a Memory

1984

When now is a memory
So hard to explain
Our time together
Pleasure or pain

When now is a memory
Be it happy or sad
My heart remembers
What yesterday had

When now is a memory
Special days like today
We embrace the moment
Before it slips away

Until the End of Time

2013

Not so long ago on Mother's Day, I sat on my bed as my mom read to me. She was reading a Mother's Day newspaper column I wrote for her.

I smiled as I looked at her face and listened to her voice read my words. Mom paused, wiped tears and said, "Honey, thank you so much, this is beautiful."

For three decades I've shared our precious moments in print. I cherish our lifetime of memories. From being six-years-old and wearing matching outfits (she made us), to coloring side by side, playing with baby dolls, or Play-Doh; our sacred memories live in my heart. To this day the smell of new crayons, dolls, or Play-Doh takes me back 50 years and reminds me of my young mommy.

When I became a mother I understood and loved my mom even more. When my daughters, Brandy and Misty were born, my mother helped me. She was always there to lend a hand and give unconditional love. My girls and my mother were very close.

118

Their nana had a huge influence in their lives. Nana reminded the girls to say their prayers and to have good manners. Nana taught them the true meaning of family. Best of all, the girls will carry on Nana's holiday traditions long after I'm gone. Brandy and Misty were blessed to share their childhood, teenage years, and their twenties with their precious nana.

There were many good times and priceless girl vacations with my mom in Big Bear, California. Tears filled my eyes after a vacation or a Mother's Day with my mom. I knew I would miss her, but I also knew I would miss her more someday.

Someday is here. This Mother's day, my dear Dolores, my mother, my friend, my confidant and my counselor is at home, happy in Heaven. Daily, I think of her and our long distance phone calls, our train rides, our car trips, our walks and our talks.

Mom told me, "The best gift you can give anyone is your time." It's true. She gave me quality time. She was never too busy for me or my girls. She was a remarkable woman. My mother sewed, cooked delicious meals and desserts, she even painted.

My multi-talented mother also made keepsake quilts and crocheted unique (one of a kind) afghans. Mom made an assortment of incredible Christmas crafts. Her breathtaking Christmas wreaths were my favorite. My mom made and gave a variety of heartwarming homemade gifts to family, friends, and charities; she gave her heart.

My mother was a wonderful woman. She didn't use profanity, and she objected when her loved ones had a "garbage mouth." She loved Jesus, was involved in her church and bible study. She adored her family and friends. My mother will forever be beautiful inside and out.

I continue to see my mother everywhere. I see her sitting in the passenger seat of my car. I see her standing next to me at church singing, holding my hand. One Sunday tears rolled down my face. I knew one day I'd have to let her soft hand go. She told me, 'Cynthia, honey, don't torture yourself. You must be strong."

I knew this Mother's day would come. I knew I'd feel a knot in my throat as I wrote, and I knew she would be reading this from Heaven. But, I also knew I'd feel better after I wrote it because sharing her life is keeping her loving spirit alive.

"Happy Mother's Day," God bless mothers and grandmothers everywhere. Thank you Mother, and like you told me, "I love you until the end of time."

About the Author

Writing is Cindy Santiago's first love and has been this author/poet's best friend as far back as she can remember. As a little girl in Waterloo, Iowa, Cindy wrote letters to people she missed.

Through the years, Cindy's numerous letters to local newspaper editors' generated interest in her writing. The editor of the Chula Vista Star-News offered Cindy a weekly column. Her *From the Heart* column ran nearly 20 years.

Cindy's stories, poems, and blogs were featured in the Imperial Beach Eagle and Times, The San Diego Christian Classifieds, and the Imperial Beach Patch. Her *Reflections* column ran five years in the Imperial Beach Sun.

Cindy lives in Imperial Beach, California with Jr., her husband of 40 years. She has two daughters; Brandy and Misty, as well as two granddaughters; Salina and Dena.

Daily, Cindy thanks God for her blessings. She hopes her words will help lost souls find their way.

About the Illustrator

Dena McLaine is only 9 years old. She has a passion for drawing and calls herself an "Anything Creator." Her family is important to her and she adores spending time with them. She loves cooking and baking, especially baking cookies. Dena has a special connection to animals. She has two dogs and a hamster and is very interested in becoming a veterinarian when she is older.

To Reach Cindy

Write to:

P.O. Box 881

Imperial Beach, CA 91933

Email: onegod2love@gmail.com

Facebook: facebook.com/cindy.santiago.7330

Made in the USA
San Bernardino, CA
01 July 2016